Soundaround

Soundaround

Developing phonological awareness skills in the Foundation Stage

Andrew Burnett and
Jackie Wylie

Illustrations by Jackie Wylie

David Fulton Publishers
London

David Fulton Publishers Ltd
The Chiswick Centre, 414 Chiswick High Road, London W4 5TF

www.fultonpublishers.co.uk

First published in Great Britain in 2002 by David Fulton Publishers

Note: The right of Andrew Burnett and Jackie Wylie to be identified as the authors of this work has been asserted by them in accordance with the Copyright, Designs and Patents Act 1988

British Library Cataloguing in Publication Data
A catalogue record for this book is available from the British Library.

ISBN 1-84312-001-1

Designed and typeset by Kenneth Burnley, Wirral, Cheshire
Printed and bound in Great Britain by Bell and Bain Ltd, Glasgow

Contents

Acknowledgements

The original Soundaround project was developed by:

- Andrew Burnett – Chief Speech and Language Therapist (Education), Plymouth Primary Care Trust.
- Mary Fry – Teacher, Mount Wise Nursery, Plymouth.
- Jackie Wylie – Specialist Speech and Language Therapist, Education Action Zone, Plymouth.
- With support from Bunty Baxter – Literacy Support teacher, Education Action Zone, Plymouth
- Administrative support – Tina Boon, Plymouth Primary Care Trust.

The Soundaround project team were grateful for the support of the Plymouth Early Years Development & Child Care Partnership, Plymouth Education Action Zone and Plymouth Primary Care Trust.

The authors wish to express their sincere thanks to all the children and adults in Plymouth who have enjoyed the games and helped them to improve the activity sheets included in this book.

About Soundaround

Why has this book been written?

Soundaround is a result of collaborative work between Early Years teachers and speech and language therapists in Plymouth. It has been developed as a resource for teachers, nursery nurses, assistants, and speech and language therapists working with children at the Foundation Stage, because, first, important links exist between early language and literacy skills development, and second, most current published resources do not offer a comprehensive and practical programme of work at this level.

What does Soundaround provide that other programmes don't?

Soundaround takes account of the 'Stepping Stones' and other advice in the *Curriculum Guidance for the Foundation Stage* (QCA 2000). The practical ideas in Soundaround will help the practitioner address the question raised by the Foundation Stage Curriculum – 'What can I actually do with the children to help them develop this skill?' Soundaround gives a more complete and systematic approach to developing a full repertoire of phonological awareness skills.

How do you use this book?

The games outlined in Soundaround are designed to help young children develop early phonological awareness skills in a fun and interactive way. The primary focus has been to provide practical, useful, and easy to follow game ideas which can be incorporated into group time in nursery and reception classes.

Who can Soundaround be used for?

Soundaround activities have not been exclusively designed for children with speech and language difficulties. Acquiring phonological awareness skills is a challenging task for all children. The developmental guidance and the record-keeping forms in this book will help practitioners select activities to suit the needs of all the children in their group/s.

What skills does Soundaround cover?

The ability levels within Soundaround reflect a developmental progression, beginning with the understanding of basic concepts and moving through to more advanced skills such as identifying first, middle and end sounds in words and developing understanding of onset and rime.

Some early sound production skills have also been included.

The Soundaround activities are divided into the following skill areas:

- Developing understanding of some basic 'concepts' underlying phonological awareness.
- Developing awareness of syllables in words.
- Developing awareness of rhyme.
- Developing awareness of sounds.
- Developing awareness of starts, ends and middles of words.
- Developing early awareness of letters/symbols.

Concepts

The ability to listen for sounds in words depends on the child having developed understanding of various 'concepts' such as;

- What is a 'word'?
- What is a 'sound'?
- What does 'start' and 'end' mean? (Other concept vocabulary such as 'first', 'last', 'beginning' can be introduced at a later date.)

It is generally assumed that the understanding of related concepts is in place at Foundation Stage. However, this is frequently not the case and direct modelling and teaching of such concepts is a necessary pre-cursor to higher level skills such as identifying start and end sounds.

Syllables

Segmenting words into syllables is an important skill for the development of literacy and can be introduced at a young age. Research has shown that syllable segmentation develops before rhyme awareness and the ability to identify initial sounds in words (Stackhouse and Wells 1997). Syllable awareness games are therefore brought in at an early stage in this manual.

Rhyme

Exposure to nursery rhymes is important but is not necessarily sufficient for a child to understand the concept of rhyme. More specific games which involve pairing and odd-one-out can be brought in at nursery level and used to model and talk about words that rhyme or 'sound almost the same'. Rhyme play can also be a useful and practical way of illustrating the reality of rhyme – hence games like 'Fabby Wabby'!

Sounds

Once children understand the concept of a 'sound' versus a 'word' they can be encouraged to listen for individual speech sounds and discriminate them from one another. They can also begin to associate that sound with a letter or picture symbol (depending on what system the school uses) and relate that sound to starts, middles and ends of a sequence of sounds.

Starts, middles and ends of words

Once children understand the concepts they can be encouraged to identify words starting or ending with the same sound. End sounds are included early in Soundaround because some children initially find it easier to listen for and identify end sounds in words.

Soundaround summary

- Suitable for all children at the Foundation Stage.

- Can be easily adapted for use at Key Stage 1.

- Based on normal development of phonological awareness skills.

- Graded activities linked to simple progress record sheets.

- Comprehensive programme of skills learning.

- Related to Curriculum Guidance.

- Original teaching ideas used by teachers, nursery nurses, playgroup staff, and speech and language therapists.

- Photocopiable activity sheets for games.

How to use Soundaround

How do I introduce sounds and letters?

Sounds are introduced at different levels (see 'Soundaround programme levels', p. 7), the order largely relating to normal speech sound development (although we do treat vowel sounds differently for practical teaching reasons). An advantage of this approach is the avoidance early on of work on sounds that some young children find difficult to identify or say. Soundaround omits work on 'q' and 'x' altogether, these two letters actually corresponding to the sound blends /kw/ and /eks/.

There is often a temptation to introduce all sounds and all letters early on, but for young children this is unnecessary and can interfere with the development of consistent sound discrimination skills and understanding of the concepts necessary for true phonological awareness.

What if the children find it hard to remember?

In Soundaround a limited range of letters is introduced early on, linked to their equivalent sounds. Letterland or other symbols that create a bridge between sounds and letter recognition can be used, particularly for children who are struggling to learn and remember new sound/letter associations. Use of these symbols can be phased out as the children progress with letters then used in their place. The symbols should always be referred to by their sound names, avoiding the situation where children learn names for characters such as 'Dippy Duck' rather than the sound itself.

Should I use sounds or alphabet names?

HEALTH WARNING!

When teaching phonological awareness skills to young children you are expecting them to become more aware of the sounds and sound structures of words. *It is very important that you consistently talk about the SOUNDS that the children can hear during the Soundaround activities rather than the letter names.*

The English spelling system is extremely confusing for young children and it should not be tackled during this vital introductory phase. Consistent reference to and use of sounds and sounds in words will help the children to understand the concepts and principles on which the spelling system is based.

Remember that only approximately 30 per cent of English words demonstrate sound–letter correspondence – in words such as 'cat' and 'dig'. Most words start or end with a different sound than you would expect from the spelling. For example, 'shoe' begins with the letter 's' but the /sh/ sound, 'knife' begins with the letter 'k' but the /n/ sound and 'house' ends with the letter 'e' but with the /s/ sound.

To remind you to use the sounds that the letter makes we have used 'forward slashes' to identify sounds in the text, for example /a/, /sh/, /y/. Also, when you say the sounds for the children to listen to, be careful not to add an 'uh'. As an example of this, the letter 's' makes a /s/ sound, not 'suh', and the letters 'sh' make a /sh/ sound, not a 'shuh'.

Where do I start in the programme?

At the beginning! You could do a screening assessment of basic skills but in many ways it is simpler to start at a level where children experience success and where activities are fun before moving on to the next level. The group leader can then continue to reinforce activities at an early level while selecting other activities at a higher level, for example the children may cope well with the early syllable work at Level 1 and be able to progress to Level 2, but need to continue with reinforcing basic conceptual understanding.

How do I record the children's progress?

There is a 'Progress record' included in the Soundaround appendices (p. 55), and this lists all the graded skill areas that are targeted. The progress record is a simple visual system, also serving as a record of ongoing assessment.

All the games are listed on page 7 – 'Soundaround programme levels'.

Each game is allocated to an ability level (1–4) and the goals of the games are outlined. Manual page numbers and progress record reference letters (A–M) are listed for each game, making a straightforward link between the games, the level of ability and how to record the children's progress.

Example: The game 'Silly Words' is for work at Level 1 on the concept of a 'word'. When the children demonstrate understanding of this activity, you record progress in column A on the progress record under 'concept awareness'. The 13 rows on the form allow you to keep simple records for individual children.

Are there any other practical considerations which I should bear in mind?

Working in a circle, letters will not always be recognisable if seen upside down or from different angles. In addition to the classic errors with confusions of 'p', 'b' and 'd' you should also be aware that 'f' and 't' can be confused, as can 'n', 'u' and 'c', and 'm' and 'w'. In some of the activities we have tried to limit this effect by ensuring that the group leader presents letters linearly. This is another reason why systems such as Letterland can be useful. The best advice is 'be aware'!

What size groups is Soundaround best suited for?

The activities in Soundaround have been designed for use with groups of up to 13 children, to correspond to the recommended adult-to-child ratio.

How have other Early Years settings used Soundaround?

It should be clear that Soundaround can be used in a variety of ways, to suit individual settings. Some examples from settings that have included Soundaround in their programme should help to demonstrate this:

- The nursery that piloted Soundaround have a group work session (13 children per group) in the morning and the afternoon. Twice a week the teacher and the nursery nurse run a 15–20-minute Soundaround session for the older children, usually involving two activities. These are sometimes recaps of a previous session, to reinforce and check on the understanding of new ideas. Activities are used at other times as session 'fillers', or on request!

  Interestingly, the themes of the activities sometimes enter the conversation or general sessions quite spontaneously – the awareness and generalisation we always hope for!

- A number of nurseries and reception classes are using Soundaround as a focus for small group work during the week, including a variety of children who are struggling with formal literacy work, also those with speech and language needs. All report significant progress in the children's understanding, raising self-esteem and leading to ability and motivation to tackle literacy in all subjects, topics and life skills.

Can I use these activities for older pupils, to include those with speech and language difficulties?

The activities can easily be adapted for use with children at Key Stage 1. For example, they can be used during word level work in the literacy hour where more challenging tasks are not yet appropriate.

They can also readily be used for other small group work, to include support work for children with specific speech and language/phonological awareness/literacy difficulties.

Soundaround programme levels

Level	Goals	Examples of suitable activities	Page	Progress Record reference
1	Concepts – sound, word, start, end, middle	Start!	9	A
		In the Middle (Level 1)	10	A
		Noisy Puppet	11	A
		Silly Words	12	A
		The End of the Line	13	A/B
	Introduction to syllables	Syllablobs	14	E/F
	Early sound knowledge – p b m w t d s f n c/k sh only	Simple Soundaround	15	B
		Puppet Says	16	B
		At the End	17	A/B
	Introduction to sound–letter links	My Turn!	18	B
	Nursery rhymes	Finish the Rhyme	19	K
	Rhyme play	Name Game	20	M
2	Syllables Level 2	Sorted!	21	E/F
		Syllable Steps	22	E/F
	Sounds knowledge – add: a e i o u	Towers of Sound	23	D
	Sounds knowledge – add: g l y h	Saved by the Sounds!	24	C
	Sound–letter links and sequencing	Two for You	25	C
	Discrimination of easy word starts and ends	Sick of Sounds	26	G
		Go to Town	27	I
	Rhyming play	Fabby Wabby	28	M
	Rhyming comparisons	Rhymers go Shopping	29	L
3	Concepts – middle	In the Middle (Level 3)	10	A
	Syllables	Hear It, See It!	30	E/F
	Sounds knowledge – add: z r v ch j	Saved by the Sounds!	24	C
	Sound sequencing – vowels via VC work	Cross the Lake	31	D
	Discrimination of starts and ends in vowel–consonant words (Seat Swap) and harder words	Seat Swap	32	D/H
		Silly Sandwiches	33	H/J
		Shopping for Sounds	34	G/H
	Rhyming comparisons	Rhyme Detectives	35	L
	Rhyming play	Monster Sounds	36	M
		Sicky Icky	37	M

Level I

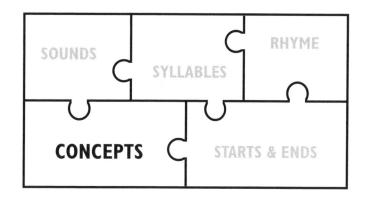

SOUNDS · SYLLABLES · RHYME · CONCEPTS · STARTS & ENDS

Title

Start!

Learning to . . .

Understand the meaning of the concept 'start' (and 'end').

Things you need

No equipment.

What to do

Explain that you are all going to do a 'Mexican Wave'. You, the leader, are at the 'start'. When you stand up, the next person copies you, and so on around the circle (establish the direction beforehand!).

For variations you could wave or put your hands up, or something easy.

Talk about the 'start' and take turns to be at the 'start'. At a later stage show how the wave goes to the 'end'. Emphasise the words 'start' and 'end' as the wave progresses.

Start!!!

Level 1

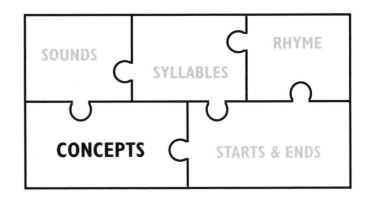

SOUNDS   SYLLABLES   RHYME

CONCEPTS   STARTS & ENDS

Title

In the Middle

Learning to . . .

Relate the concept 'middle' to the use of sounds.

Things you need

•   A small selection of sound symbol cards.

What to do

Game 1 (Level 1)

Ask three children to stand up and then ask the other children to decide who is in the middle. You could reinforce this concept with a simple rhyme such as 'Hey diddle diddle, s/he's in the middle!'

Game 2 (Level 3)

Ask three children to stand up and each choose and hold up a sound symbol card. Adult says the three separate sounds, starting from the left, and then asks 'What sound is in the middle?'

Game 3 (Level 4)

Ask three children to stand up, the first and third to choose a consonant symbol card, the middle child to choose one of the vowel cards. Ask the circle 'what sound is in the middle?' As an introduction to sound blending, slowly say the word the children have made, for example, '/t/- /a/- /k/, that makes tak!' You can informally talk about any real words that are formed.

Level 1

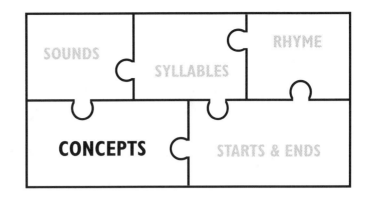

SOUNDS   SYLLABLES   RHYME

CONCEPTS   STARTS & ENDS

Title

Noisy Puppet

Learning to . . .

Understand the concept of a sound and discriminate sound from silence.

Things you need

•   Two puppets.

What to do

One puppet tells the other to go to sleep as he has to go out. He asks the children (or one child if you are taking turns around the circle) in the group to listen very carefully to the sleeping puppet to check whether he makes a sound or not, as he tends to be very noisy in his sleep.

The puppet leaves and the children or child listens carefully. Sometimes the sleeping puppet will make loud sounds, sometimes quiet, sometimes funny sounds and sometimes speech sounds (for example /s/, /t/ etc.). Sometimes the puppet will remain silent until the other puppet returns. When the other puppet returns he asks if he has made a sound. If the puppet has made a sound the child must wake him and tell him, but if he has been silent the child must let him sleep.

Level 1

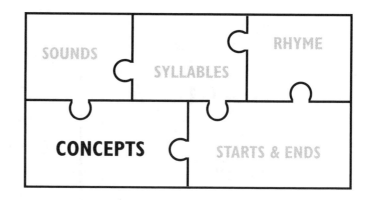

SOUNDS   SYLLABLES   RHYME

CONCEPTS   STARTS & ENDS

Title

Silly Words

Learning to . . .

Understand the concept of a word and identify real and silly words.

Things you need

- Two packs of prepared cards. Half the cards have real words (such as table, sweets) written on them. The other cards have nonsense words (such as clob, snud) written on them. The second pack of cards has corresponding pictures on the back of the real word cards, and crosses on the back of the nonsense word cards.
- Puppet and a box for the cards.

What to do

The leader explains that puppet has a load of cards in his box. Some of them say words we all know, like 'car' and 'mummy', but some of them have 'silly' names – they are not words. (Follow the children's lead if they start to talk about 'real' or 'pretend' and so on.)

The leader picks up a card from the words-only pack, says the word on it and asks, 'Is that a word?'

The children can check their answer when the leader picks the corresponding card from the second pack and turns it over (usefully done by a second adult).

At the end, do a review – and then puppet puts the silly words 'in the bin'!

Level 1

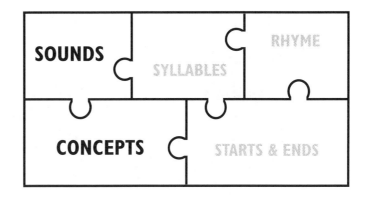

SOUNDS · SYLLABLES · RHYME

CONCEPTS · STARTS & ENDS

Title	**Learning to . . .**
The End of the Line	Reinforce the concept 'end' and relate it to a simple sound sequence (this activity could also be used to work on the concept 'start').

Things you need

- A circle of train track, e.g. Duplo, arranged around the inside of the circle.
- A train plus a few trucks.
- Sound symbol cards.

What to do

Push the train round the track and stop it in front of someone (who is listening and looking quietly?). Say something like 'The train stopped by Jack – let's see who is down the end of the train'. 'Katie is down the end!' 'Katie' then chooses another child who is sitting quietly and the train is pushed round to them.

The introductory exercise can be left out once the children are used to the game format.

Next, warn the children that they will hear a special sound down the end of the train when it stops again. You can make a neutral 'train' noise as the train moves, then stop the train and continue the noise while you pass your hand down the length of the train. When your hand reaches the end truck, make a speech sound. The child at the 'end' is expected to repeat the sound you have made, or point to a symbol card representing the sound.

Level 1

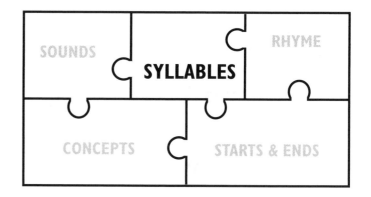

SOUNDS · RHYME · **SYLLABLES** · CONCEPTS · STARTS & ENDS

Title	**Learning to . . .**
Syllablobs	Work out the number of syllables in a word, e.g. rabbit = 2!

Things you need

- Two syllablob cards – one for the leader, one for the children.
- Pictures/objects of things with 1–2 syllables, moving on to 3–4-syllable words as the children's understanding increases.

(1–2)	(3)	(4)
dog, lorry, sausage	dinosaur, computer, banana	caterpillar, television

For examples of 1–4 syllable words see 'Syllable word lists' (Appendix A, p. 45).

What to do

The children take turns choosing a picture/object.

They use the syllablob card to help them work out the number of syllables /'bits' as they say the name.

The children point to the blobs, moving from left to right, as they say the word.

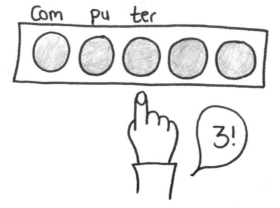

How many blobs/bits/syllables? Three!

Level 1

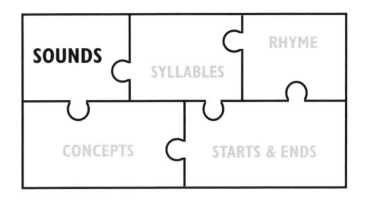

SOUNDS · SYLLABLES · RHYME · CONCEPTS · STARTS & ENDS

Title

Simple Soundaround

Learning to . . .

Identify single sounds.

Things you need

You may wish to talk about the sounds first. Select two or more, dependent on the experience of the group – and say the sounds as you show the corresponding letter cards.

What to do

See above for preparation.

Allocate sounds to individual children, e.g. if /p/, /f/ and /s/ are used, the first child has to remember /p/, the second /f/, the third /s/, the fourth /p/ and so on. Follow the format of the circle time game 'Fruit Basket' – the children have to swap places when their sound is said. In this game, the 'All change' command 'Fruit Basket' would become 'All the Sounds'.

The circle leader could pass the role of leader to children who are listening particularly well. Watch out for sounds that some children can't say as leader.

Level I

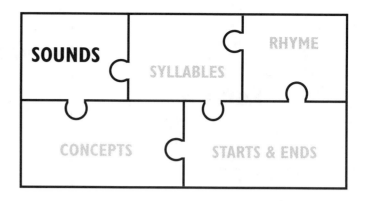

SOUNDS | SYLLABLES | RHYME

CONCEPTS | STARTS & ENDS

Title

Puppet Says

Learning to . . .

Listen for a sound (sounds) and begin to discriminate different sounds and relate them to the letter or picture symbol.

Things you need

- Puppet.
- Sound/letter cards in a bag.

What to do

Introduce the puppet to the children and say that he is going to be the 'leader' in a game.

To choose a sound you could ask a child to pick a sound symbol or letter card out of a bag. Practise making the sound together. Make up an action for the sound. For example, move your arm like a long snake for the /s/ sound, pretend to bang a drum for the /d/ sound, etc. Any actions can be used or you can use Nuffield or Letterland symbol-related actions. Do this for a number of sounds pulled from the bag. The more sounds, the harder the game – so start with three and work up.

Play 'Puppet Says'. The puppet says a sound and the children have to do the action. You can try to catch the children out by making the puppet say other sounds too (some speech sounds and some silly non-speech sounds). Remember that the more similar the distraction sounds are to the target ones, the harder it will be for the children to discriminate, e.g. /sh/ when the target is /s/ would be very difficult.

At a later time or date you can introduce letters/symbols which the children are encouraged to point to when puppet says the appropriate sound – gradually phase out the actions.

Level 1

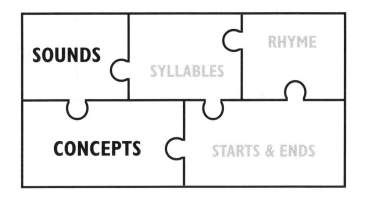

SOUNDS SYLLABLES RHYME
CONCEPTS STARTS & ENDS

Title

At the End

Learning to . . .

Relate the concept 'end' to the use of sounds.

Things you need

- A 'magic wand' or similar.
- Two or more sound symbol cards.

What to do

The adult introduces the magic wand, which moves round the circle, stopping occasionally and pointing at one of the children.

As the wand moves 'it' makes a neutral sound, e.g. humming. The children are warned that when it gets 'to the end' it will make a speech sound and they will have to listen and then find the correct sound card. Learners can just repeat the sound or be given forced alternatives to help them. Reinforce the idea that the sound was 'at the end'.

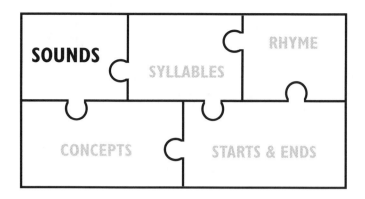

Title

My Turn!

Learning to . . .

Identify easy speech sounds and relate them to symbols.

Things you need

* A pack of symbol cards (Letterland symbols are a useful bridge to subsequent use of letters, but other systems can also be used).
* Use only a few sounds to start with, for example select from /f s t p k sh/.

What to do

By way of an introduction talk about the cards and the sounds they represent, exaggerating the sounds and using any associated gestures (which are usually related to the visual symbol you are using). For example, talk about keeping quiet and put your finger to your lips as you discuss the sound /sh/. (See the section 'How to use Soundaround' (p. 4) for more details).

When first playing the game, use a pack of cards with just a few card types, e.g. /sh/, /t/, /p/.

You should also lay one example of each card on the floor/table.

To start the game the adult picks a card and, without letting the circle members see the card, makes the appropriate sound, e.g. /sh/. One of the children is chosen and has to guess which card on the floor represents the sound made. If right, they keep the card. If wrong, you could help them, using a forced alternative, for example 'Was it /f/ or /sh/?' (pointing to the appropriate cards as you say these sounds).

Level 1

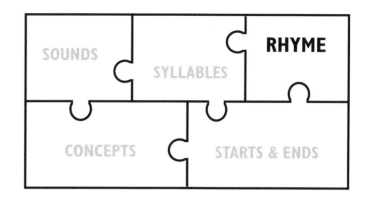

SOUNDS SYLLABLES **RHYME**

CONCEPTS STARTS & ENDS

Title

Finish the Rhyme

Learning to . . .

Identify and remember the rhyming words in nursery rhymes.

Things you need

- Puppet
- Nursery rhymes.

What to do

Sing or say nursery rhymes, using a 'forgetful' puppet who sometimes forgets to say the rhyming words, for example:

'Jack and Jill

went up the . . . ?'

Variations

Sometimes the puppet could accidentally put in the wrong word!

'Jack and Jill

went up the stairs!'

Remember to talk about how some of the words sound almost the same – they rhyme!

Level 1

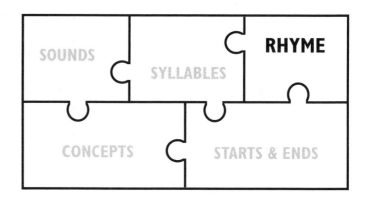

SOUNDS · SYLLABLES · **RHYME** · CONCEPTS · STARTS & ENDS

Title

Name Game

Learning to . . .

Recognise a rhyming string of two words.

Things you need

No materials needed but you may like to use a picture or puppet to introduce the concept of rhyming with a name, e.g. 'Humpty Dumpty' or 'Dirty Berty' etc.

What to do

Introduce and model rhyming words, e.g. by using a puppet called 'Dirty Berty' or 'Curly Shirley' etc. or a familiar nursery rhyme character like 'Humpty Dumpty'. Talk about how you are going to make a silly rhyme – a word that nearly sounds the same – out of everyone's name.

Go round the circle, taking each child in turn and thinking of a rhyme, e.g. 'Smiley Kylie', 'Blue Sue', 'Slack Jack', 'Still Bill' etc. Nonsense words may also be used if you can't think of a real word that rhymes, e.g. 'Filliam William' etc.

Smiley Kylie   Curley Shirley   Magid Ragid

Can the children help you to think of the rhymes?

Finally, review the names and emphasise how they 'nearly sound the same' . . . they rhyme!

Level 2

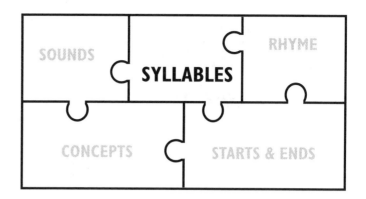

SOUNDS | SYLLABLES | RHYME

CONCEPTS | STARTS & ENDS

Title

Sorted!

Learning to . . .

Sort words according to syllable number.

Things you need

*   Mixture of pictures or objects with 1–3 syllables, e.g. hat = 1; a..pple = 2; am..bu..lance = 3 etc. (see 'Syllable word list' (Appendix A, p. 45) for examples)
*   3 hoops
*   Picture of one dot, two dots, three dots (to represent syllable number).

What to do

Mix the pictures face down on the floor in the middle of the circle (or put the objects in a bag and shake them up). Explain that they are a mess and need to be sorted out. Put the hoops on the floor and put one dot in one, two dots in another and three dots in the other (or use written numbers 1–3).

The leader may need to model the game first a couple of times, then the children take turns to choose a picture or object, clap and say the word and put it in the right hoop for the number of claps or beats in the word. E.g. hat = one clap, am..bu..lance = three claps, etc. If the child needs help, clap and say the word with them at first.

Check the words together at the end by clapping and saying them.

If clapping doesn't work, use Syllablob cards.

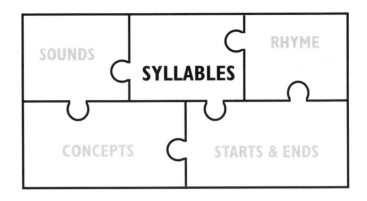

SYLLABLES

Title

Syllable Steps

Learning to . . .

Recognise the number of syllables ('bits') in words or sentences.

Things you need

• You could use cut-out footprints arranged around the inside of the circle, one in front of each person.

• A list of suitable words (1–4 syllables long) e.g. ball, Sophie, crocodile, caterpillar, etc. This can either be a word list or a mix of pictures that the children choose from (see 'Syllable word lists' (Appendix A, p. 45) for examples).

What to do

Choose a child. They stand up and listen to a word (or pull a picture from a hat or pile). They have to move along the footprints the right number of steps to match the number of syllables in the word, e.g. three syllables = three steps. (All?) say the word as the child moves along, stressing the syllables, e.g. 'Cro..co..dile'.

The child then swaps places with the child sitting opposite where they stop.

As the children get used to the game they can join in choosing and saying the words.

Level 2

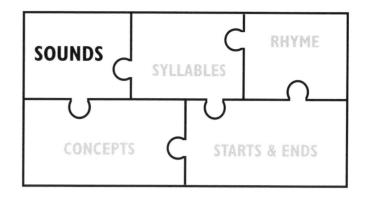

SOUNDS

SYLLABLES

RHYME

CONCEPTS

STARTS & ENDS

Title

Towers of Sound

Learning to . . .

Listen for the vowel sounds in isolation and match them to the written letters or symbols.

Things you need

Sound/letter cards for the vowels a, e, i, o, u.

What to do

Start by introducing two contrasting vowel sounds, for example /a/ and /i/. Put the sound/letter cards in the middle of the circle.

Bring in a puppet and tell the children that this puppet REALLY likes saying these sounds /a/ and /i/ and wants to check whether the children are all listening today (or have got their ears switched on).

Give each child a building block or Lego® brick.

The puppet then tells them that he wants them to help him build two really tall towers – the /a/ tower and the /i/ tower. When he says /a/ they must put a brick on the 'a' and when he says /i/ they must put a brick on the 'i'. The bricks go on top of each other to build a tower. You can ask the children to guess which one will be the tallest or which one will fall down first as you play.

The children take turns listening for the puppet's sound and putting a brick on the corresponding tower.

Level 2

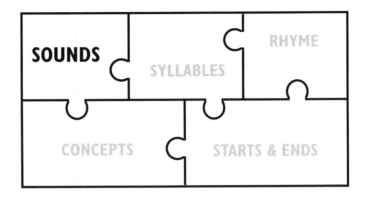

| SOUNDS | SYLLABLES | RHYME |
| CONCEPTS | STARTS & ENDS | |

Title

Saved by the Sounds!

Learning to . . .

Match sounds to letters/symbols.

Things you need

- 'Dragon' puppet or similar.
- Letter/symbol (e.g. Letterland) cards for each pupil. Initially give each pupil two sound cards.

What to do

Dragon is very keen on sounds and letters and wants to check that the children know all about them too – or else!

Dragon sings/hums a song quietly to the children but occasionally he says a sound. The children must hold up or point to the card representing that sound so that dragon can check it. If it's the wrong card they get told off (nicely!), and the correct answer is modelled by the other children.

Note – start with easy sounds such as /sh/ and /t/.

Children still learning the sound–letter links will be able to copy the others initially.

Variations

Sound cards could be put on 'desert islands' arranged on the floor around the room. Play a version of 'Pirates' so that when the children hear a sound they have to run to the island with that sound on it, before the crocodile/dragon gets them.

A good way to finish the session if the children have spent a lot of time sitting down!

Level 2

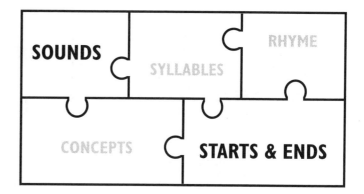

SOUNDS · SYLLABLES · RHYME · CONCEPTS · STARTS & ENDS

Title	**Learning to . . .**
Two for You	Identify two spsoken sounds in sequence (this is an introduction to starts and ends of words).

Things you need

• Sound–letter cards spread around the centre of the circle.

What to do

The leader says two sounds and the next pupil has to find the two corresponding cards, standing on them in the same order that they were said. If they find the correct cards, but in the wrong order, say the two sounds again and get them to step on them 'the same as I say them'.

Gradually introduce the notion of 'start' and 'end' as the child identifies the cards.

Variations – do the splits between the cards. You can also do a table-top version of the game, pointing to the cards.

Who can do three sounds? (HARD!). Probably use for Level 3/4.

Level 2

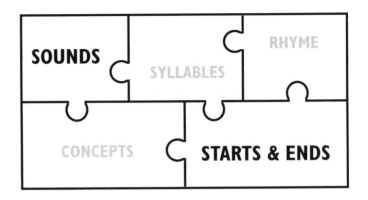

SOUNDS · SYLLABLES · RHYME

CONCEPTS · STARTS & ENDS

Title	**Learning to . . .**
Sick of Sounds	Identify the start sounds in words.

Things you need

- Posting boxes – animals starting with two different sounds, e.g. snake and lion.
- Optional 'bag of food'.
- Pictures beginning with the /s/ and /l/ sounds (or whatever sounds your animals' names begin with).

What to do

Introduce the posting boxes. Give the animals names beginning with their sound, e.g. Sammy Snake, Lenny Lion etc.

Explain that the animals are hungry and want the children to help feed them – but they are fussy eaters and will only eat things that start with the same sound as their name. You may choose to use letter/picture symbol cards to remind the children of these sounds.

The children then take it in turns to take food pictures from a bag or pile and feed them to the right animal. If they make a mistake model the error, e.g. 'Is it a ssssolly? or a lolly?' etc. To make the game harder, include pictures of food which do not begin with either sound (these then go in the bin or cupboard). The animals can eat 'silly' things. At the end the animals can be 'sick'. Empty the boxes and go over what they have eaten, emphasising the start sounds.

Level 2

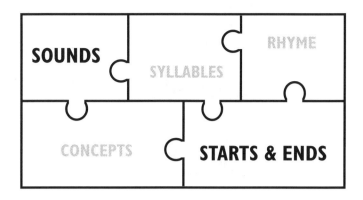

SOUNDS

SYLLABLES

RHYME

CONCEPTS

STARTS & ENDS

Title

Go to Town

Learning to . . .

Identify the end sounds in words and match words with the same end sound.

Things you need

Pictures of 2–3 different modes of transport ending in different sounds, e.g. bus, train, bike. Pictures of people with names ending in one of the two or three sounds on the end of the transport words (in our version /s/, /n/, /k/ sounds)

What to do

Put the 2–3 transport pictures on the floor in the middle of the group and name the items. Emphasise the end sound of the word. You may like to put a letter by each to remind the children of the end sound.

Put the pictures of people face up in the middle and explain that you need the children's help to make sure the people get to town. Explain that the children have to go in or on the thing that ends with the same sound as their name. Give the children an example by choosing one of the pictures and looking at their name (written on the back). Say the name and emphasise the end sound, e.g. 'Mar..k..' Talk about the end sound being /k/ and ask the children to spot which transport has a /k/ sound on the end. Model how the words end in the same sound, e.g. 'Yes, so Mar..k.. goes on the bi..ke' etc. Remember, it is sounds and not letters that we are focusing on (e.g. Monique would go on the bike!). Each child then has a turn to choose a person and put them in the right place. You will need to say the names of the people for the children and emphasise the sound on the end as you do so.

Do the children's names work?

Level 2

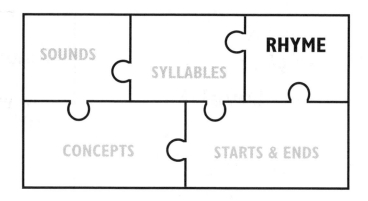

SOUNDS
SYLLABLES
RHYME
CONCEPTS
STARTS & ENDS

Title

Fabby Wabby

Learning to . . .

Play with rimes, identifying the same 'end bits' and 'rhyming bits' of nonsense and real words.

Things you need

- A list of easy 'rimes' that all (or most) of the children will be able to say. Two syllable forms are often easier to hear/remember initially, e.g. 'abby', 'oppy', 'icky'.
- Sound/letter cards.

What to do

If you have selected e.g. 'abby', say this three times and then get the children to join in.

Explain that you are going to add a sound to the start of the word, for example /f/. Show the card at the same time. Do 'fabby' three times and then get the children to join in. Demonstrate that the end bit is not changing, e.g. 'fabby . . . abby'.

Continue with a few different sounds.

Variations

Children can do it in turns round the circle, or do it with friends on their turn – e.g. first child says the sound /f/ and second child says 'abby' – then put the sounds together to make 'fabby' etc.

Introduce the idea that the same 'end bits' are rhyming. At the end, run through all the 'words' you have made.

Level 2

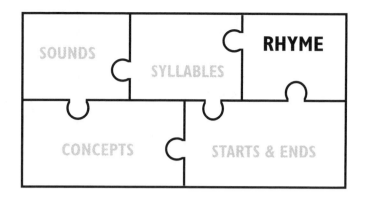

SOUNDS
SYLLABLES
RHYME
CONCEPTS
STARTS & ENDS

Title	**Learning to . . .**
Rhymers go Shopping	Match rhyming words.

Things you need

- Pictures of food items.
- Pictures of 'monsters' or strange characters.

What to do

Lay out three pictures of food items and explain that the children are going to take turns to be shopkeepers. When someone comes into their shop they will want to buy something that rhymes with (or sounds a bit the same as) their name. Give an example, e.g. bring in a picture of Mr Fleeze and have a choice of bread, cheese and milk. Ask the children what they think Mr Fleeze is going to buy, e.g. 'Is Mr Fleeze going to buy some milk?', 'Is Mr Fleeze going to buy some cheese?' etc. Remind the children that they need to find something that rhymes with his name.

Bring in a new character for each child and give them a choice of three food items to choose from. If a child finds rhyming difficult, using multi-syllabic words may make the rhyme easier to hear, e.g. 'Mrs Tewcumber' buys some cucumber. If they get the right rhyming word they can win the character. At the end, go over all the rhyming pairs you have found.

Level 3

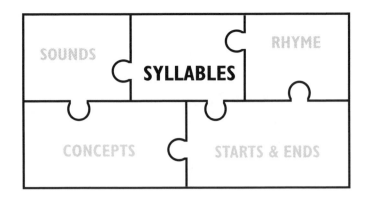

SOUNDS SYLLABLES RHYME

CONCEPTS STARTS & ENDS

Title

Hear It, See It!

Learning to . . .

Find words around the room with 1–4 syllables.

Things you need

- No equipment needed but you may choose to use the 'Syllablobs' card or a visual prompt to help the children count syllables rather than clapping alone.
- See 'Syllable word list' (Appendix A, p. 45) for examples of suitable words.

What to do

Remind the children about syllable beats in words – clapping the word and/or using the 'Syllablobs' card or visual cues. You will have already done lots of work on syllables before doing this game.

Explain that you are going to clap the syllables of something in the room and the children have to see if they can guess what word it might be. Take turns around the circle giving everyone a chance to guess.

Clap 1–4 claps and ask the child to find something in the room with that number of claps. If the child gets it right, model it for the rest of the group (by clapping and saying or using the syllablobs card), e.g. 'a...pple' is two claps, 'bu...ter...fly' is three claps, etc. If they find this hard you can make it much easier by offering them a limited choice, e.g. pointing out two or three things with different numbers of syllables.

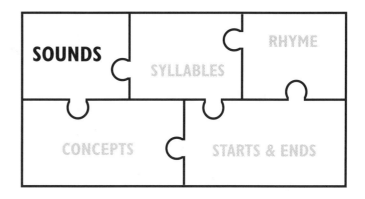

SOUNDS — SYLLABLES — RHYME — CONCEPTS — STARTS & ENDS

Title

Cross the Lake

Learning to . . .

Identify letters to match vowel sounds and introduce sequencing of vowels and consonants.

Things you need

• Letters/symbols for vowel sounds and consonant sounds.

What to do

Choose two vowel sounds at first, e.g. /a/ and /u/. Talk about these sounds and relate the sound to the letter. Lay a selection of /a/ and /u/ cards on the floor at random and then add other consonant sounds (limit the choice at first to two, for example /d/ and /sh/). Explain that the middle of the circle is a dangerous lake and the children are going to have to cross it. They must put their feet on the sounds they hear. If they do not, they may get eaten by the monster of the lake. If you have space you may like to sit in two rows facing each other rather than a circle.

One child stands up and listens to the sounds you say. Start with a vowel sound and sequence vowel then consonant until the child is across to the other side, e.g. /a/ . . . /s/ . . . /u/ . . . /d/ . . . /u/ . . . /sh/ . . . /a/ . . . /d/ etc. If the child gets it wrong you can choose whether they get eaten or not but don't make getting eaten too much fun or all the children will want to fail! When they get to the other side everyone claps and a child from that side then has a turn to get across. As the children get better at this they can take turns to be teacher and you can introduce more vowel and consonant sounds to choose from.

SOUND AROUND

Level 3

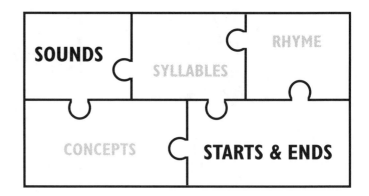

SOUNDS | SYLLABLES | RHYME

CONCEPTS | STARTS & ENDS

Title

Seat Swap

Learning to . . .

Identify vowel sounds at the start of easy VC words.

Things you need

Three or four of each of the letters 'a', 'e', 'i', 'o', 'u' written on card (or use symbol cards such as Nuffield or Letterland).

What to do

Spread the cards evenly around the centre of the circle. The leader chooses two children to stand up. They have to listen to the leader say one of the following words:

At   Egg   In   On   Up

The children have to identify the vowel sound at the start of the word and then stand on the appropriate letter. The leader then says the other words at random and the children step from one letter to the next, aiming to get closer to the seat (or space) of their partner – eventually reaching it!

A good tip! Use just two vowels the first few times you play this game, adding the others as the children become more confident.

Level 3

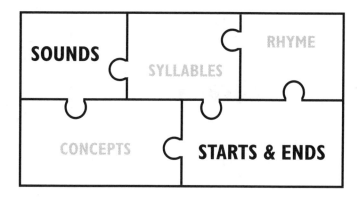

SOUNDS

SYLLABLES

RHYME

CONCEPTS

STARTS & ENDS

Title

Silly Sandwiches

Learning to . . .

Identify sounds at the start (or ends) of words.

Things you need

- Two cardboard bread shapes, to make a sandwich.
- A selection of pictures of food items plus 'silly' things such as shoe, worm, sock and bucket.
- Sound/letter cards.

What to do

Place a selection of the food cards and 'silly' items in the centre of the circle. Also put the appropriate sound/letter cards on view somewhere in the circle.

Explain that you are going to make sandwiches for each other.

The first player chosen by the leader closes his/her eyes. The leader picks a food or 'silly' card and puts it in the sandwich.

All the other children say 'Ready' and the first player opens his/her eyes, pretends to eat the sandwich and then says if it was 'nice' or 'horrible'. The player is then allowed to look inside the sandwich – an animated discussion about what is nice or horrible is guaranteed to take place!

Finally, the player who 'ate' the sandwich has to decide what sound is at the start (or end) of the word.

If necessary, the other players can help, following which the next member of the group has a turn.

TIP: Use cards starting (or ending) with a limited range of sounds (two or three?) when you first play this game, for example /p/, /s/ and /k/ only.

Level 3

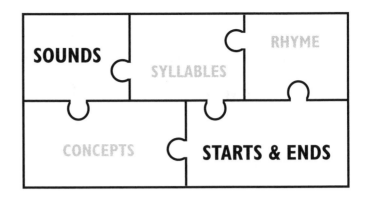

SOUNDS · SYLLABLES · RHYME · CONCEPTS · STARTS & ENDS

Title *Shopping for Sounds*	**Learning to . . .** Identify the start sounds of words.

Things you need

- Shopping basket.
- Pictures/objects with a selected range of start sounds.

What to do

Each child in the circle is given one or more pictures/objects to look after. One child is given the shopping basket and a starting sound written on a card.

They walk to another child and ask 'Have you got something starting with (their sound)?' and continue until they get something and check the answer.

The child who gives an item then becomes the shopper, using the same or a new sound card.

Carry on!

Review what sounds and linked items have been 'used' at the end of the shopping trip.

Level 3

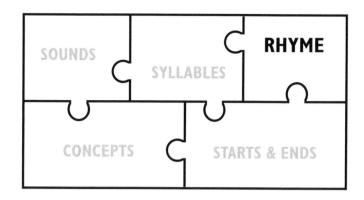

SOUNDS SYLLABLES **RHYME**

CONCEPTS STARTS & ENDS

Title

Rhyme Detectives

Learning to . . .

Identify rhyming pairs.

Things you need

- Rhyming pictures or objects. Either pairs or sets of four, six (easier and faster game if more than two words rhyme in the group) etc. E.g. cat . . . hat . . . bat . . . fat . . . / bear . . . chair . . . hair, etc.
- Shopping basket.

What to do

Each child is given a picture or object. Make sure all the children know what their picture or object is. Make sure the leader has some spares to give out later.

One child takes the shopping basket and goes round the circle to find a word that rhymes with theirs. You can encourage the child to say their word and each child they go to round the circle has to say their own word back to them, e.g. 'cat' . . . 'chair'. The leader then asks – 'Do they rhyme?' or 'Do they sound almost the same?' If they do, the child puts the picture or object into their basket and keeps them. The basket is then given to the child who gave their picture or object away and the leader gives them a new picture or object. The game continues.

At the end of the game, go through 'what rhymes' in the basket.

Level 3

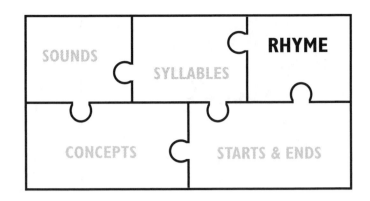

SOUNDS

SYLLABLES

RHYME

CONCEPTS

STARTS & ENDS

Title

Monster Sounds

Learning to . . .

Understand that the rhyming ends of words stay the same – and that changing the start sounds creates new words.

Things you need

Pictures or puppets of monsters who have the names: 'inky', 'appy', 'olly', 'oddy', 'eggy' or similar! (these two syllable forms tend to be more memorable than single-syllable ends/rimes such as 'it' or 'at').

What to do

Introduce the monsters by their names and explain that they like to play with sounds and put them at the start of their own names – just to see what happens!

The adult puts a letter/sound symbol to the left of the monster and says the two in sequence, for example /p/ + 'inky' makes 'pinky'! After doing a few more from letters suggested by the children, e.g. 'tinky', 'winky', 'binky', talk about the new names you have made – but the 'inky' bit is still there on the end. They rhyme!

Variations

As the children become more familiar with the activity, include more sounds and do group chants of the products, e.g. /b/ + inky . . . ' binky binky binky'!

You could also begin to show the rhyming pattern by chanting 'binky winky' etc.

Level 3

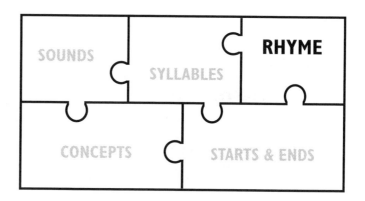

SOUNDS
SYLLABLES
RHYME
CONCEPTS
STARTS & ENDS

Title

Sicky Icky

Learning to . . .

Change the first sound of a word to make a new rhyming word.

Things you need

- Picture symbols or letters to represent initial sounds and a selection of monsters (hand drawn is fine!).
- A bag or a box.

What to do

Introduce a monster called 'Icky' to the group. Explain that Icky wants help from the children to find new 'words' that rhyme with his name. Show the children a bag or box, which has a selection of letters or picture symbols to represent letter sounds inside. Pull a letter from this bag/box and ask the children to tell you what sound it makes. Then demonstrate how you can put that sound onto the start of Icky's name to make a new word, e.g. 'k..k..kicky', 'ssssss..sicky' etc. Model the rhyme, e.g. 'Kicky Icky', 'Sicky Icky' and put the letter to the left of the monster, pointing left to right to emphasise the start and end of the word. Talk about how these words rhyme.

The children take turns to pull a letter from the bag or box. After you have done a few for Icky introduce a new monster, e.g. called 'Unny', 'Appy', 'Izzy' etc. Continue to model the rhyme and emphasise how changing the first sound makes a new silly word. N.B. Two-syllable forms (such as 'icky', 'olly' etc.) tend to be more memorable than single-syllable 'ends' such as 'it' or 'at'.

Level 4

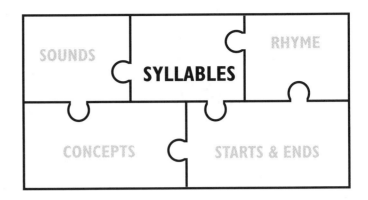

SOUNDS

SYLLABLES

RHYME

CONCEPTS

STARTS & ENDS

Title

Words Go Round

Learning to . . .

Identify and produce the syllables of a multi-syllabic word.

Things you need

A list of common words, for example, crocodile, computer, video, Natalie, to include some two-syllable words so you can start at an easy level e.g. Sophie, button, carrot (see 'Syllable word lists' (Appendix A, p. 45).

What to do

Say a two-syllable word and really emphasise the syllables, e.g. 'So-phie', 'Ja-son'. Now explain that you will say the first 'bit'/syllable and the person next to you has to say the second syllable.

If necessary, do this with another adult in the circle, otherwise go round the circle using the same word: 'So-phie, So-phie . . .' If there are an odd number of people in the circle, try going round more than once – you will then 'change syllables' on the second time round!

If the children can easily manage two-syllable words, change to three-syllable words such as: com-pu-ter, cro-co-dile. To avoid confusion, do not move on too quickly – the progression to 3–4-syllable words may take several weeks.

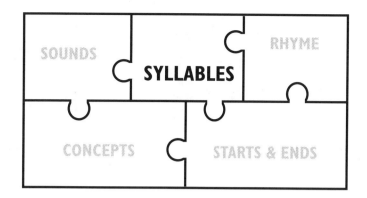

SOUNDS

SYLLABLES

RHYME

CONCEPTS

STARTS & ENDS

Title

Clap and Snap

Learning to . . .

Make judgements about syllable number without having to say the words aloud.

Things you need

Picture pairs 1–3 syllable words (see 'Syllable word lists' (Appendix A, p. 45)).

What to do

The leader has one set of the pictures and the others are kept on one side. Each child has a turn listening to the leader clapping (but not saying) the syllables of one of the pictures. The child has to find the picture from a choice of three (one syllable, two syllables or three syllables). For example, target picture = bed. Choice for child = bed (target), spider (two syllables) and banana (three syllables). Adult claps once (since bed = 1 syllable). Child selects bed then claps it and says it to check they are right. All children can join in the clapping and saying of the word to see if the child was right. Give them two turns if necessary and let them 'keep' the card if they are right.

You can make this harder by increasing the choice of pictures.

Level 4

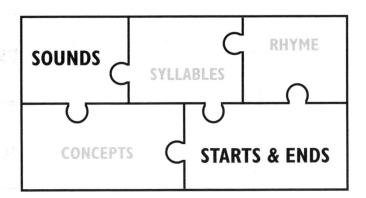

SOUNDS · SYLLABLES · RHYME · CONCEPTS · STARTS & ENDS

Title	**Learning to . . .**
Where's the Sound?	Identify where you hear the sound – is it at the start or the end of the word?

Things you need

- A selection of pictures, the words starting or ending with targeted sound(s).
- Letters or symbols to represent the sound(s) being listened for.
- Picture of a train with an engine and carriages, or another item with an obvious start and end.

What to do

Choose one sound at first, e.g. /s/. Have a selection of pictures that start or end with the /s/ sound (e.g. sun, sandwich, house, grass, race etc. – remember it is the 'sound', not the letter, that is important).

Put the pictures in the middle of the circle.

Explain that the children are listening and looking for the /s/ sound. If they hear the /s/ at the start of the word, they are going to put the picture at the start of the train (i.e. the engine). If they hear the /s/ at the end of the word they are going to put the picture at the end of the train.

If the child gets it wrong you can model their mistake, e.g. mouse → start of train – 'Hmmm, is it a sssssouse?' (as you run your finger left to right along the train). If they are stuck offer a choice, e.g. 'Is it ssssouse or is it mousssse?'

Once the children are good with one sound you can increase the choice of sounds at the start and end.

Level 4

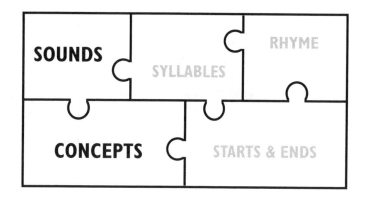

| SOUNDS | SYLLABLES | RHYME |
| CONCEPTS | | STARTS & ENDS |

Title

Hungry Monsters

Learning to . . .

Identify the vowel sound in a CVC word.

Things you need

- Letters/symbols for the vowel sounds /a/, /i/, /e/, /o/ and /u/.
- Pictures of CVC words.
- Pictures of monsters with mouths (or puppets or boxes with faces on).

What to do

Introduce two monsters (at first) to the children. The monsters must have CVC names where the vowel sound is the one you are targeting, e.g. if you choose to target /i/ and /a/ first your monsters could be called 'Hig' and 'Hag'.

Explain that the children are going to help you feed the monsters as they are hungry; however, they are very fussy and they only eat things that have the same sound in the middle as their names. Talk about their names and emphasise the middle sound for the children to hear.

Introduce the letters to match the middle sounds and put them with each monster. The children then take turns to choose a picture of a food item from a bag (it doesn't have to be edible as monsters can eat anything, and the more silly, the better). They then have to decide if the food goes to Hig or Hag according to what sound is in the middle. Model any errors, e.g. 'Hmm if Hag eats it, it must have the /a/ sound . . . chaps . . . is that right? No, it's chips so it must be the /i/ sound' etc. At the end the monsters can be sick and you can go over what they ate! Introduce more monsters for the other vowel sounds when the children are familiar with the game.

Level 4

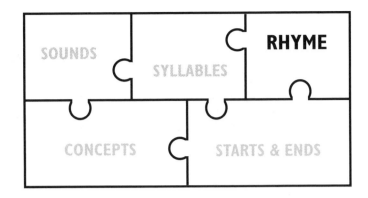

		RHYME
SOUNDS	SYLLABLES	
CONCEPTS	STARTS & ENDS	

Title

Wammy, Bammy, Sammy

Learning to . . .

Create a rhyming string by changing the first sound of the word.

Things you need

- Selection of letters/symbols to represent sounds.
- Word endings such as 'ammy', 'unny', 'acky', 'appy' etc. written on card.

What to do

Show the children a word-ending card, e.g. 'ammy'. Read it and ask the children to say it with you. Put a selection of letters in the middle of the circle face down (being careful that you exclude any that may create an unsuitable word when put on the start of the chosen word ending). Explain that the 'ammy' is only the end of the word/the rhyming bit and the children are going to find different start sounds and make new words.

Demonstrate by picking up a letter card. Say the sound that the letter makes. Then say the sound at the start of the word, holding up the letter and 'ammy' for the children to see. E.g. '/t/ – if I put it at the start of the word I can make a new word /t/..ammy, /t/..ammy, that makes "tammy".' Each child takes a turn around the circle to pick up a hidden letter and make a new rhyming word. Help if necessary by modelling, e.g. '/d/..inny, /d/..inny, that makes "dinny" – can you say that?' Stress how all the 'words' you are making rhyme. If a child makes a 'real' word they can have another turn. At the end of the game review all the rhyming 'words' you created round the circle.

Level 4

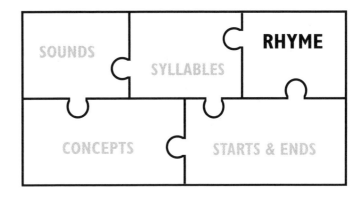

		RHYME
SOUNDS	SYLLABLES	
CONCEPTS	STARTS & ENDS	

Title

Cat Hat Fat Bat

Learning to ...

Understand that changing the first sound of single-syllable words creates new rhyming words and learning to blend onset and rimes.

Things you need

- Single-syllable word endings (rimes) written on card, e.g. 'at', 'un', etc.
- Sets of four rhyming pictures that match the written word endings on card (for examples see Appendix B, p. 48).
- Letters/Sound symbol cards for the corresponding first sounds of the rhyming words in the sets.
- A puppet.

What to do

Introduce a puppet to the children explaining that he likes to make new words.

The puppet then chooses a card from a box or bag. This card will have a word ending written on (such as 'at'). The puppet says 'at' 'at' lots of times and then starts to yawn and says that he is really bored saying 'at' and he wants some new exciting words to say.

Put four rhyming pictures in the middle and name them (e.g. 'cat', 'hat', 'fat', 'bat').

The children then take turns to choose a letter/sound symbol card from a bag or box. These cards correspond to the first sounds of the pictured words, e.g. /k or c/, /h/, /f/ and /b/ – everybody says the sound.

Then the puppet puts the sound to the left of the 'at' card facing the child and says the sound plus the ending, e.g. 'b . . . at', 'b . . . at'. The child has to listen to the puppet and then choose which word they think the puppet has just said from the choice of pictures in the middle.

After three children have had a turn do the fourth one together as a group then talk about how all the words you have found rhyme (or sound a bit the same) because they have the same ending. Say the words together.

Get a new word-ending card for the puppet and a new set of rhyming pictures.

At the end the puppet goes over all the rhyming words he has found.

Level 4

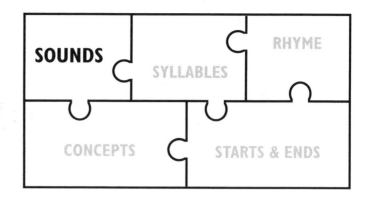

| SOUNDS | SYLLABLES | RHYME |
| CONCEPTS | STARTS & ENDS | |

Title

Puppet's Homework

Learning to . . .

Identify the two sounds in a consonant blend at the starts of words.

Things you need

• Puppet with paper and pens.
• Pictures or objects starting with different consonant blends* (two consonants).
• Letter/sound symbols to represent the sounds in the blends.

What to do

Introduce the puppet and explain that he has some tricky homework to do and he needs the children's help. He has been given a bag of sounds and a bag of words and he has to sort out which sounds go at the start of which words. The reason he's finding it so hard is that he needs to find TWO sounds at the start of the words and not just one. Empty the letters into the middle of the circle face up (start with a limited number, e.g. a choice of f, s, l, p).

Model for the children first by picking an object or picture from puppet's bag of words and naming the word, e.g. 'fly'. Emphasise the start sounds by lengthening them (*it is easier to begin listening for blends using 'long' sounds such as sss and fff and avoiding sounds that are more difficult to discriminate, e.g. 'r'). The children listen for and identify the start sound ('ff') and then listen for the next sound (emphasise the sounds as you say them). Once you have found the two letters puppet has to write them on a piece of paper. Each child has a turn and keeps their picture and the written letters to match it. Review what you have found at the end, emphasising the first two sounds.

Appendix A: Syllable word lists

One-syllable words

Toys	Clothes etc.	Animals	Transport	Food/Drink	Home etc.	Body parts	Other
Ball	Shoe	Dog	Car	Bread	Bed	Nose	Spoon
Kite	Sock	Cat	Bus	Cheese	Chair	Ears	Watch
Swing	Shirt	Mouse	Train	Milk	Desk	Eyes	Cup
Slide	Skirt	Fish	Boat	Soup	Lamp	Mouth	Moon
Bricks	Dress	Bird	Ship	Sweets	Clock	Arm	Sun
Doll	Hat	Duck	Sledge	Pear	Sink	Leg	Knife
Drum	Pants	Goat	Coach	Cake	Bath	Hand	Fork
Paint	Coat	Cow	Truck	Egg	Fridge	Foot	Star
Farm	Gloves	Sheep	Pram	Juice	Broom	Neck	Book
Game	Bib	Pig	Cart	Chips	Mop	Head	Soap
Clown	Shorts	Horse	Tank	Grapes	Shelves	Hip	Key
Spade	Cap	Seal	Crane	Crisps	Stool	Wrist	Tree
Rake	Tights	Frog		Tea	Bin	Thumb	Comb
Sand	Tie	Bear		Rice	Cot	Teeth	Brush
Stilts	Scarf	Bat		Beans	Door	Tongue	Purse
	Blouse	Fox		Peas	Roof	Lips	Plate
	Jeans	Wolf		Peach	House	Toes	Torch
	Vest	Bee		Jam		Hair	Glass
	Belt	Worm		Pie		Back	Saw
	Ring	Snail		Tin/Can		Chin	Drill
	Zip	Shark					Girl
	Bag	Swan					Boy
							Man
							Sad
							Box
							Ghost

Two-syllable words

Toys	Clothes etc.	Animals	Transport	Food/Drink	Home	Body parts	Other
Teddy	Trousers	Giraffe	Lorry	Carrot	Toilet	Finger	Flower
Puzzle	Jumper	Tiger	Spaceship	Yoghurt	Sofa / Settee	Elbow	Toothbrush
Trumpet	Tracksuit	Chicken	Rocket	Biscuit	Cushion	Shoulder	Scissors
Guitar	Jacket	Lizard	Canoe	Pizza	Pillow	Tummy	Basket
Football	Apron	Spider	Warship	Salad	Blanket	Ankle	Candle
Jigsaw	T-Shirt	Donkey	Ferry	Raisins	Oven	Bottom	Hammer
Skittles	Trainers	Rabbit	Speedboat	Chicken	Kettle	Eyebrow	Spanner
Balloon	Nightdress	Zebra	Steam train	Coffee	Hoover	Forehead	Snowman
Tea set	Slippers	Monkey	Digger	Ice cream	Curtains		Santa
Lego	Sandals	Leopard	Wheelchair	Apple	Window		Lady
Puppet	Sweatshirt	Badger	Scooter	Orange	Wardrobe		Grandma
Play dough	Sari	Hedgehog	Taxi	Hot dog	Cupboard		Granddad
Pencils	Nappy	Panda	Tractor	Peanuts	Garden		Letter
Whistle	Necklace	Squirrel		Popcorn			Yellow
Bucket	Earring	Hamster		Sandwich			Purple
Paper	Buttons	Tortoise		Water			Orange
Skateboard	Lipstick	Dolphin		Sweetcorn			Bandage
		Seagull		Baked beans			Happy
		Parrot		Sugar			Baby
		Peacock		Cabbage			Garage
		Penguin		Lemon			Bottle
		Gerbil		Cherries			Dummy
		Monster		Mango			
				Honey			
				Melon			
				Mushroom			
				Cracker			

Three-syllable words (to include associations e.g. rocking horse)

Toys	Clothes etc.	Animals	Transport	Food/Drink	Home	Other
Recorder	Cardigan	Butterfly	Bicycle	Hamburger	Frying pan	Radio
Roller skates	Dungarees	Crocodile	Tricycle	Cucumber	Microwave	Stereo
Climbing frame	Bikini	Chim-	Aeroplane	Samosa	Computer	Wheelbarrow
Roundabout	Dressing gown	panzee	Canal boat	Spaghetti	Piano	Telephone
Rocking horse	Pyjamas	Elephant	Rowing boat	Potato	Lawn mower	Umbrella
Rolling pin		Kangaroo	Submarine	Cereal		Video
Skipping rope		Ladybird	Underground	Tomato		Fishing rod
Violin		Centipede	Motorbike	Banana		Skeleton
Swimming pool		Octopus	Caravan	Lollipop		
Dominoes		Guinea	Police car	Pineapple		
Spinning top		pig	Ambulance	Coconut		
Playstation		Dinosaur	Fire engine	Aubergine		
Nintendo				Birthday cake		

Four-syllable words

Television
Caterpillar
Alligator
Rhinoceros
Calculator
Swimming costume
Radiator
Washing machine
Vacuum cleaner

Dressing table
Tape recorder
Helicopter
Tennis racket
Wellington boots
Supermarket
Coca cola
CD player
Pepsi Cola

Some confusing ones!
You decide how many syllables there are for these and other similar examples

Raspberry
Strawberry
Onion
Broccoli
Cauliflower
Camera
Lion

Appendix B:
Rhyming word pictures

Photocopiable illustrations (pages 49–54) that will be useful for a range of rhyming awareness activities to include:

- Cat Hat Fat Bat (page 43)
- Rhymers Go Shopping (page 29)
- Rhyming Detectives (page 35)

Rain	Train	Plane	Chain
Eye	Fly	Cry	Tie
Shoe	Two	Glue	Loo

Book	Cook	Hook	Look
Chair	Hair	Bear	Pear
Tea	Tree	Key	Bee

Cat	Hat	Fat	Bat
Pan	Man	Fan	Can
Sun	Bun	Run	One

Drink	Sink	Wink	Think
Knock	Clock	Sock	Rock
Frog	Log	Dog	Jog

Pin	Bin	Thin	Spin
Sing	Ring	Swing	Wing
Nail	Sail	Snail	Tail

Stick	Brick	Kick	Lick
Ball	Tall	Fall	Wall
Snake	Cake	Rake	Lake

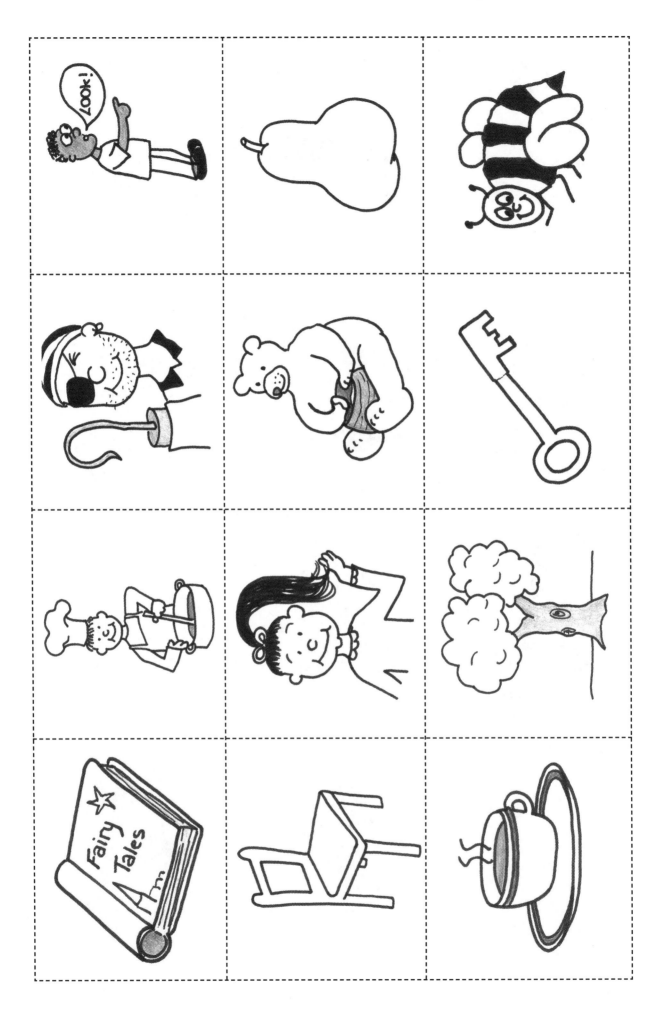

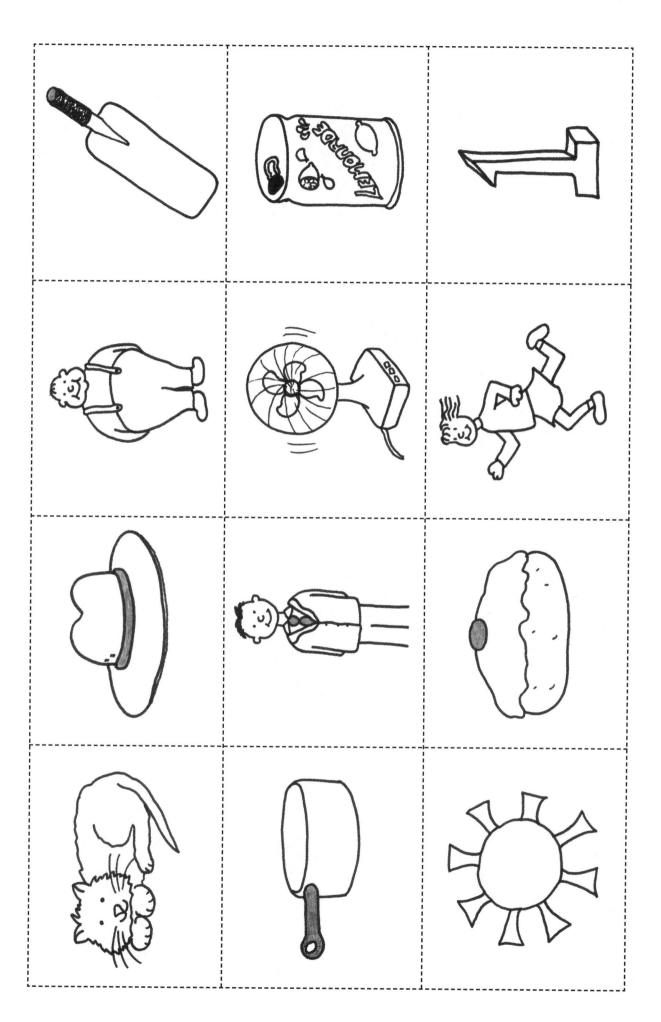

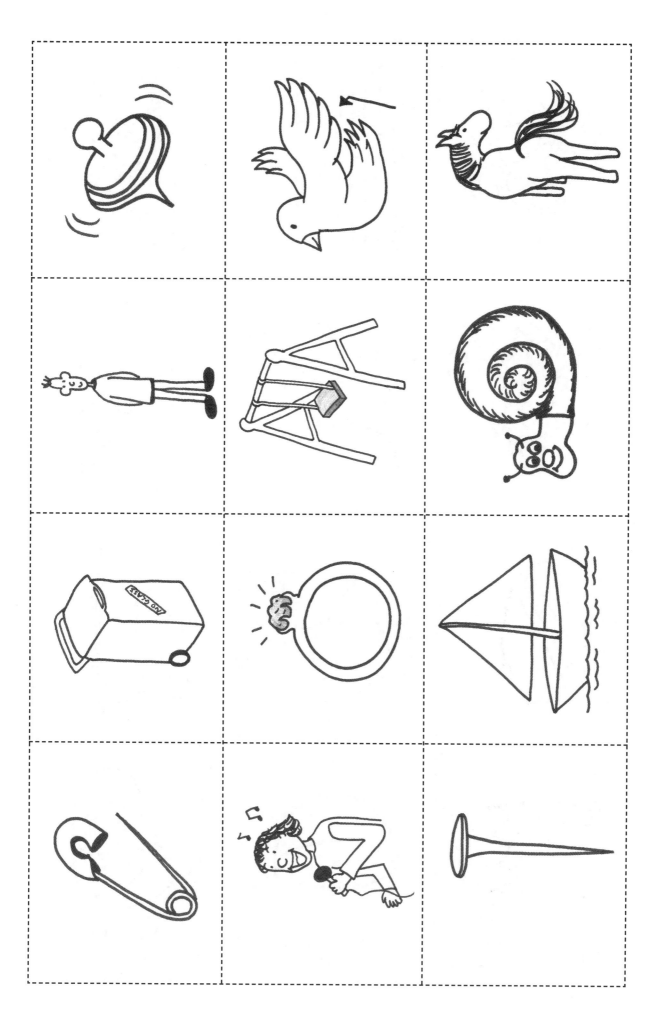

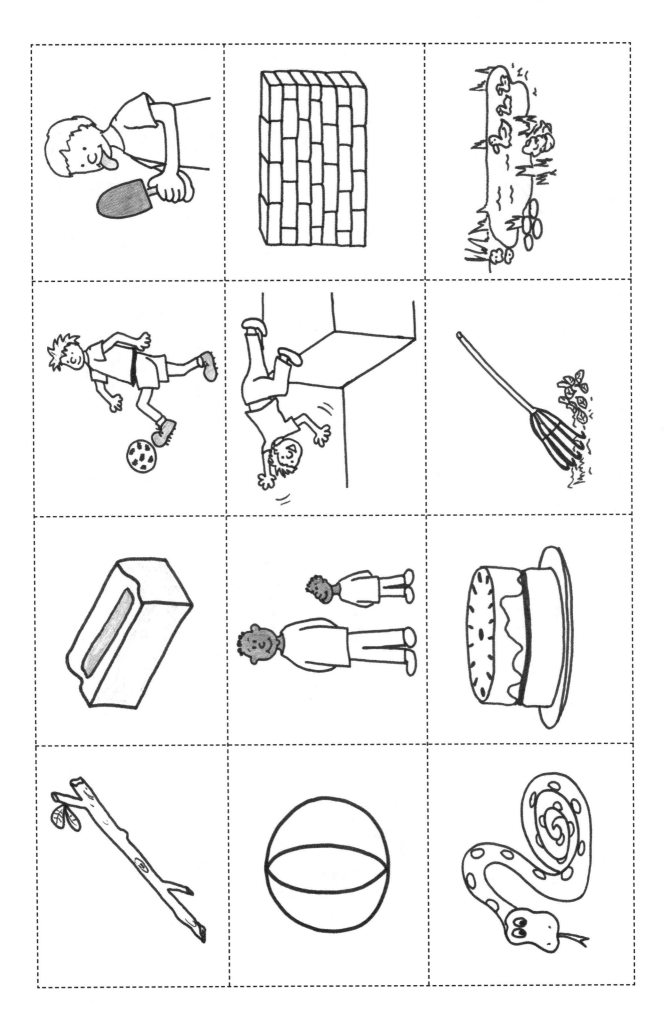

Appendix C: Soundaround progress record

Child's name	Concept awareness	Single sound Knowledge and sound/ letter links Level 1	Single sound Knowledge and sound/ letter links Levels 2–4	Vowel sounds and letter links	Syllable awareness 1–2 syllables	Syllable awareness 3–4+ syllables	Word start awareness Levels 1–2	Word start awareness Levels 3–4	Word end awareness Levels 1–2	Word end awareness Levels 3–4	Rhyme awareness easy, e.g. nursery rhymes	Rhyme awareness hard, e.g. word comparing	Rhyme production and rhyming play
	A	B	C	D	E	F	G	H	I	J	K	L	M

Skills undeveloped

Some understanding

Further understanding

Good knowledge level

Satisfactory skill level

Appendix D:
References, further reading and resources

*Catts, H. (1991) Facilitating Phonological Awareness: Role of Speech and Language Pathologists, *Language, Speech and Hearing Services in Schools*, Vol. 22, pp. 196–203.

Goshwami, U. (1994) The Role of Analogies in Reading Development, *Support for Learning*, Vol. 9 No. 1.

Gross. J. and Garnett, J. (1994) Preventing Reading Difficulties: Rhyme and Alliteration in the Real World, *Educational Psychology in Practice*, Vol. 9 No. 4.

Hurd, A. and McQueen, D. (2000) The Right Things at the Right Time, *Speech and Language Therapy in Practice*, Winter, pp. 8–11.

Layton, L. (1994) Underpinning Literacy, *Special Children*, May, pp. 15–18.

*North, C. and Parker, M. (1994) Teaching Phonological Awareness, *Child Language Teaching and Therapy*, pp. 247–57.

Qualifications and Curriculum Authority (2000) *Curriculum Guidance for the Foundation Stage*, London, QCA.

Stackhouse, J. and Nathan, L. (2000) 'The World of Words', *Special!*, Summer, pp. 8–11.

Stackhouse, K. and Wells, B. (1997) *Children's Speech and Literacy Difficulties – A Psycholinguistic Framework*, London: Whurr Publishers.

Yopp, H. (1992) Developing Phonemic Awareness in Young Children, *The Reading Teacher*, Vol. 45 No. 9, May.

RESOURCES

Bricknell, S. (1987) *Effective Pre-Reading*, New South Wales: Horwitz.

Burnett, A. (ed.) (1995) *Working Together on Speech and Reading – A Co-operative Approach for Teachers and Speech and Language Therapists*, Children's Speech and Language Service, Seventrees Clinic, Baring Street, Plymouth PL4 8NF.

Catts, H. and Vartiainen, T. (1993) *Sounds Abound*, East Moline, Illinois: Linguisystems Inc.

Delamain, C. and Spring, J. (2001) *Developing Baseline Communication Skills*, Bicester: Winslow.

*DfEE (1999) *Progression in Phonics: Materials for Whole-class Teaching*, London: DfEE.

Goldsworthy, C. (1988) *Sourcebook of Phonological Awareness Activities*, San Diego, CA: Singular Thomson Learning.

Layton. L. and Denny, K. (2002) *Sound Practice* (second edition), London: David Fulton Publishers.

Nash-Wortham, M. (1993) *Phonic Rhyme Time*, Stourbridge: Robinswood Press.

Otley, P. and Bennett, L. (1997) *Launch into Reading Success*, London: Psychological Corporation.

Wendon, L. (1997) *Letterland*, London: HarperCollins Publishers Limited.

Wilson, J. (1995) *Learning to Read with Nursery Rhymes*, London: Educational Psychology Publishing, University College.

Wilson J. (1997) *Phonological Awareness Training* (beginners book), London: Educational Psychology Publishing, University College.

ASSESSMENT

Dodd, B., Crosbie, S., McIntosh, B., Teitzel, T. and Ozanne, A. (2001) *Preschool and Primary Inventory of Phonological Awareness* (3 years–6 years 11 months), London: Psychological Corporation.